T0116443

THE MIND'S

Edict

A Plethora Of Poems

VERSE

authorHOUSE®

AuthorHouse™ UK
1663 Liberty Drive
Bloomington, IN 47403 USA
www.authorhouse.co.uk
Phone: UK TFN: 0800 0148641 (Toll Free inside the UK)
    UK Local: (02) 0369 56322 (+44 20 3695 6322 from outside the UK)

Published by AuthorHouse 01/11/2024

ISBN: 979-8-8230-8500-7 (sc)
ISBN: 979-8-8230-8501-4 (e)

Library of Congress Control Number: 2023918601

Print information available on the last page.

This book is printed on acid-free paper.

THE MIND'S EXPANSE

Within the minds expanse,

There lies truth and lies diction,

To discern and identify

Is nothing but fact and fiction,

The end in which we start

Can become a prerequisite,

But nothing less and never short

Of anything but infinite.

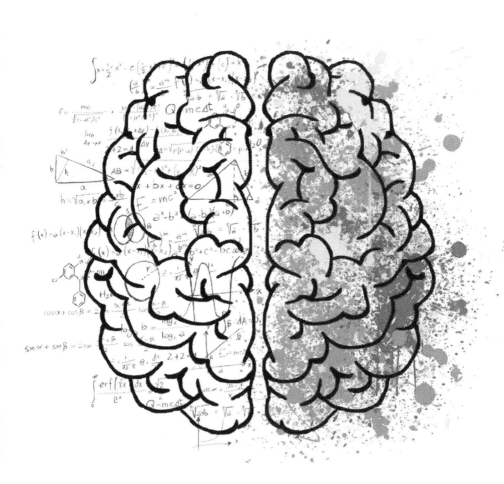

THE ANNEXES

In the annexes of the mind,

There is experience and there is fate,

That to differentiate is for one to spectate,

There can be gladness, reprieve, concern and woe,

Yet however one deems to travel, is
however far they shall go

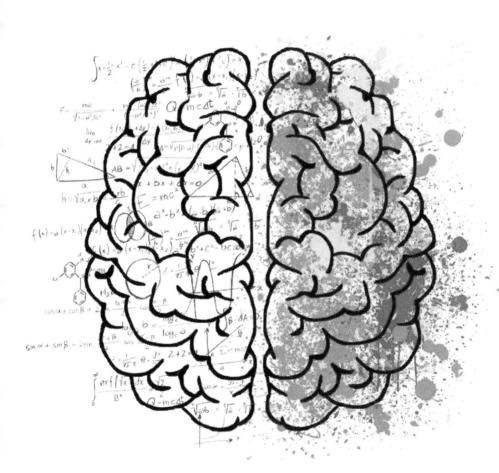

Chaos

Chaos, as begrudgingly profound, leads to conflation,
which drowns us and proclaims to astound, that which
is whole can never be complete, whilst that which is
finished begins to process that which it repeats.

Delusion and sobriety, paradoxical in nature,

Delves into the annals of imagination and procedure,
the lines of fate twisted around that which is between,
begins to emerge from the cracks that we seam.

Posture and relevance lead to beauty and coercion,
debilitating if unsought and paralytic in perversion.

The heart and the mind at battle for one, leading
he charge to whomsoever has been won.

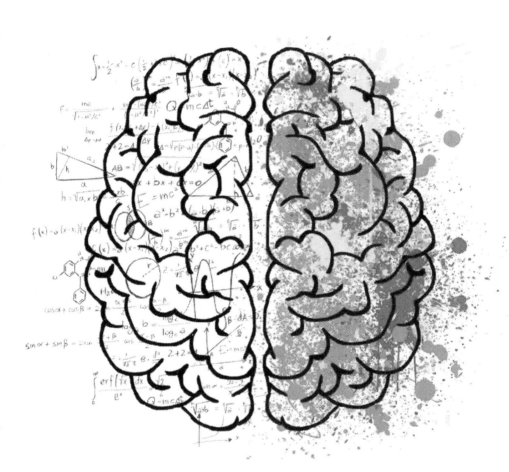

THE LUMINATED FRAY

Despite the souls yearning for effervescence, the harrowing, dimly illuminated path pertains closing frays.

Betwixt these motions of arduous and unpredictable tasks lies serenity, its goal undecided and predicted to be enumerated.

Serenity surrounds us, guides and challenges intuitive caveats to procure discernment and revelry.

This conjunctive state is delectable, deplorable and delegatory, allowing ones beats to be heard and spirit to be revered.

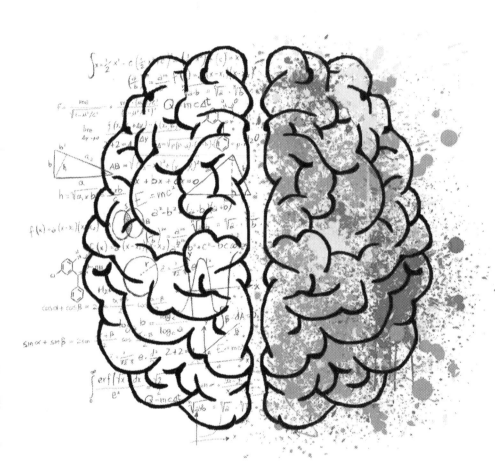

THE DELVE

The intricacies of a minds delve can upend and reconstruct one's mind, left to wither allows for the malignant.

In tandem, with procurement it can solidify one's alignment.

This besieges he hear to arouse its entropic cravings and deliver oneself from containment.

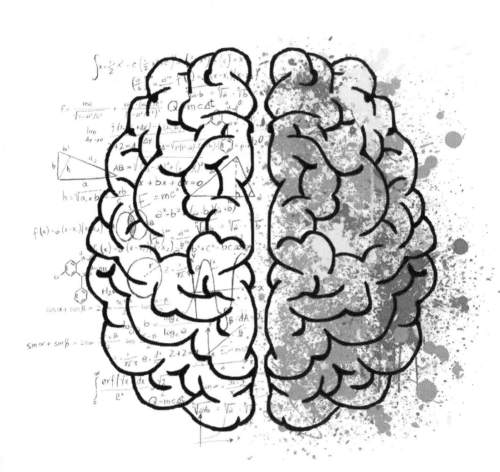

VORTICES

Within the swirling vortex of the everlasting
and distant horizon, there is peace.

The topic of belief to each being and their own.

The placidity of rigid thinking and base reality leads
to the existence of conclusive activity, allowing
one to manifest their own destiny, experience
or what you, yourself, have named It.

The differentiation of thoughts and beliefs equate to one's
own baser instincts and reliefs, to build a connection with
their own identity as well as their individual understanding.

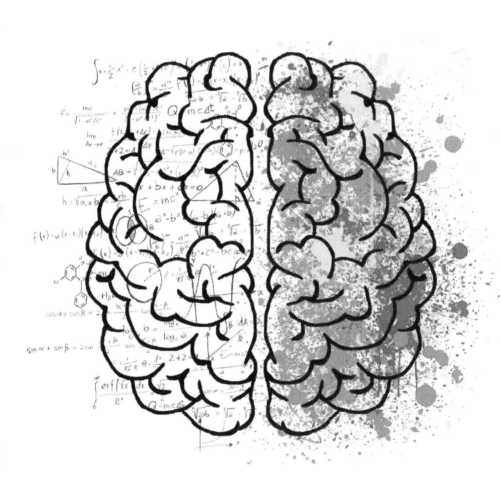

MYSTIC

Mysticism, the line between the mind and its surroundings,
he cover page for life and its arcane performance.

Begins as a whimper, progresses through
profoundness to end with sought after revelation,
the labyrinth is ever flowing and interchanging.

Plots allow for depth, schemes for deception,
plans for continuity and orders for finality.

This deliberation is the crux of the beneficiary
and the crutch to the maudlin, leaving one to
wonder to what rhythm does it beat.

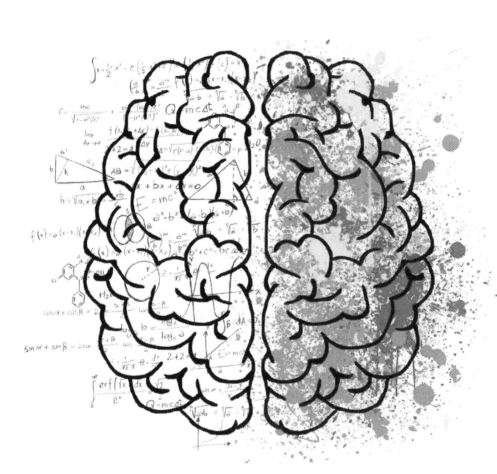

THE START?

To begin from the start is for one to know their end, yet
the challenges that are to be faced can easily upend.

Differences appear and challenges are to be sought, whilst
the answers bring peace and yet everlasting thought.

Within these philosophies one can bring to bear,
the weight of many sins balanced by a hair.

Completionists may finish,

Where perfectionists may strive,

As enablers resolve to which the thoughtless can provide.

Belligerence and honesty,

The soul of Yin and Yang,

Forever to be wed in a place of ampersands.

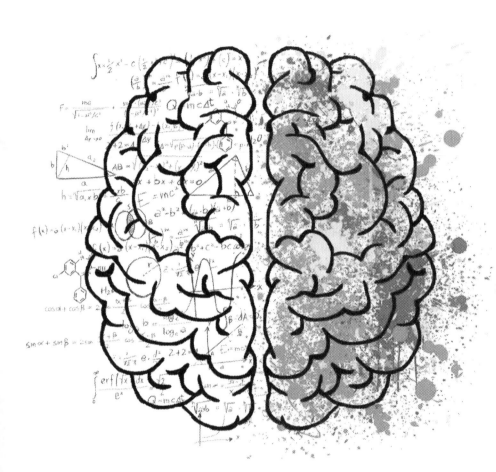

The Strive for Compassion

Relevancy and compassion,

Two ends of the spectrum of fortitude,

Bereave those of disdained collages
and compelling afterthoughts,

Colloquially calling for acknowledgement and recognition.

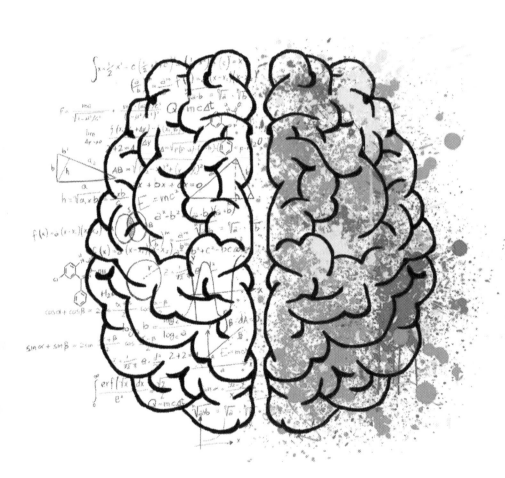

BEWONDERED

Many think to wonder,

Paces of which that blunder,

Plenty of times asunder,

Many think to wonder.

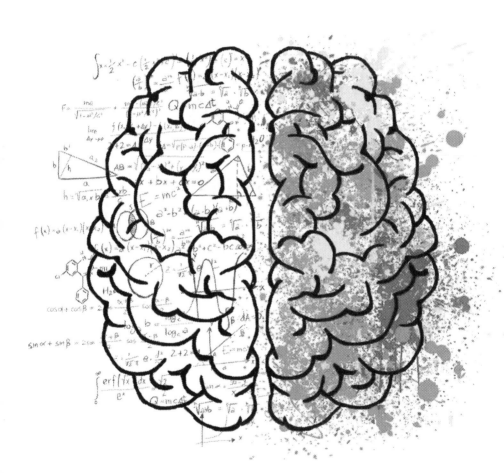

THE AFTERTHOUGHT

Derelict pastimes and converging products,

Describing reality one smidgeon to the next,

Allowing for disruption confusion and deductions,

That which passers-by will take ajar.

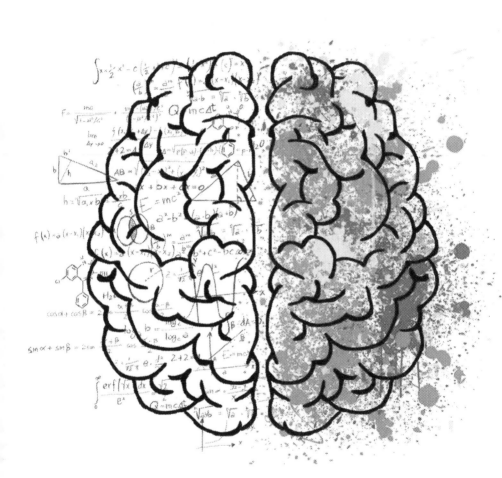

WORDING

These words lie heavy,

Spoken so light,

Depicted as a sun beam,

Hidden as the moon,

Completed by the photon,

Enlightened by the muon,

Ever interchanging the actions of the human.

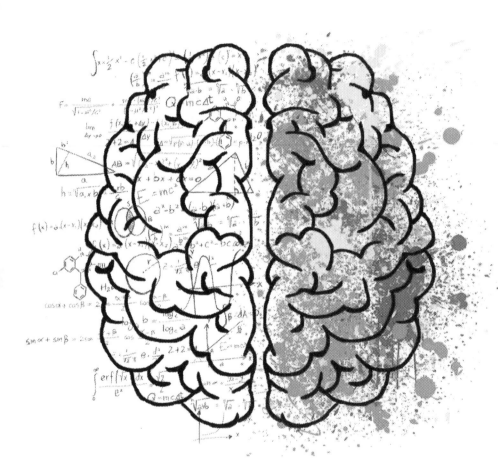

HEALTH IS YOUR WEALTH

Health is the wealth to those of the world,

Brought ever so wearily to the masses,

As blindsides and corruption seed false idols to devise,

Leaving health on the backburners solitary in strive.

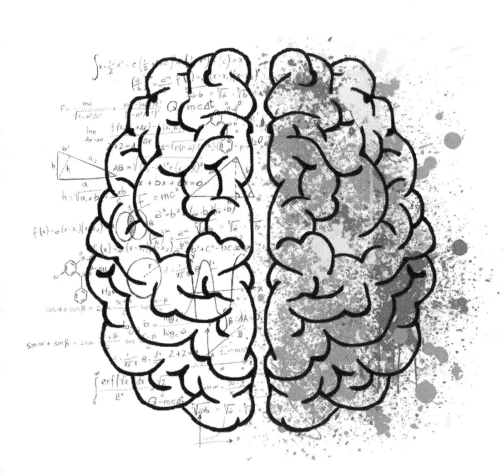

THE STARS

The stars be our guide,

Astronomically they writhe,

With lifetimes they surprise,

The lonely given eye.

Brilliance in grace an abundance of space.

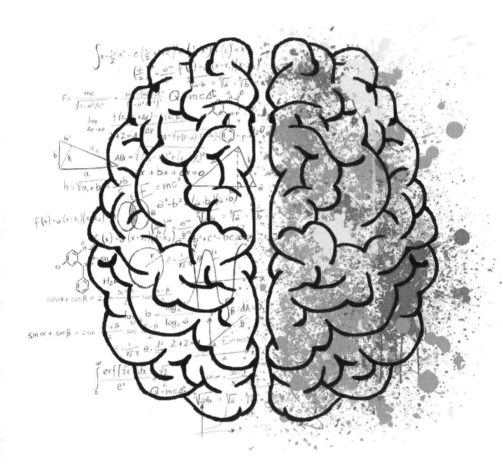

CON/TENT/TEMPT

With a bracing heart and intuitive mind,

One can interpret the heavenly divine,

Debased and defunct allow for one to understand
and challenge the morally "asinine".

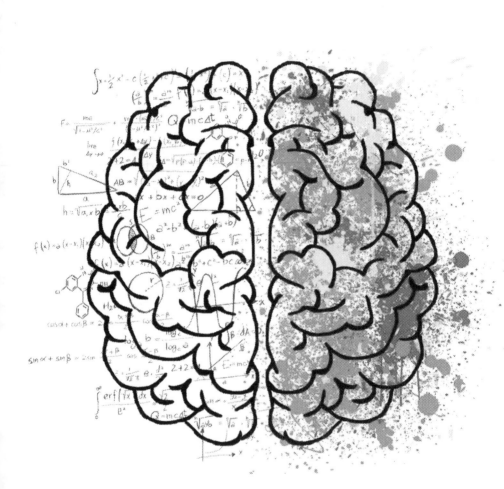

WELL?

Projection, an intriguing thought, yes?

Does it allow for conveyance?

Allow for conveyance?

Allow for conveyance?

Allow for conveyance?

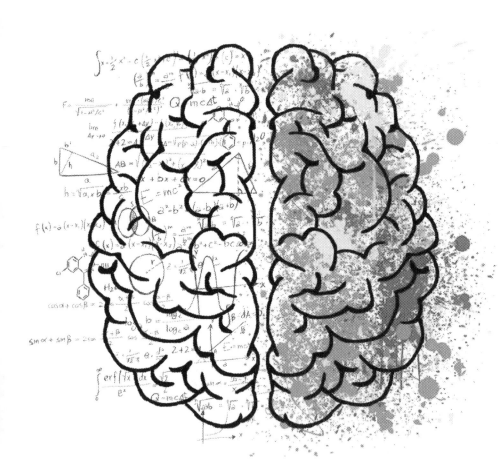

The Shine

Golden gates stand,

As one may land,

Hidden to the side is temptation with demand,

Ponder at the relevance and cease with the challenge,

Depict *your* enlightenment and seek your reprimands.

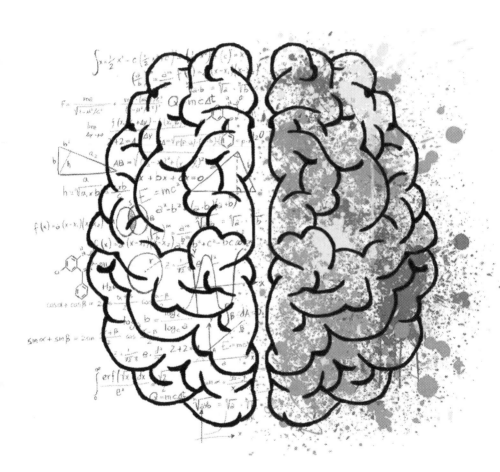

SPEAK

The sword of tongue connects the thoughts of the dumb,

Implied by the rules of thumb and
becomes the shield of One.

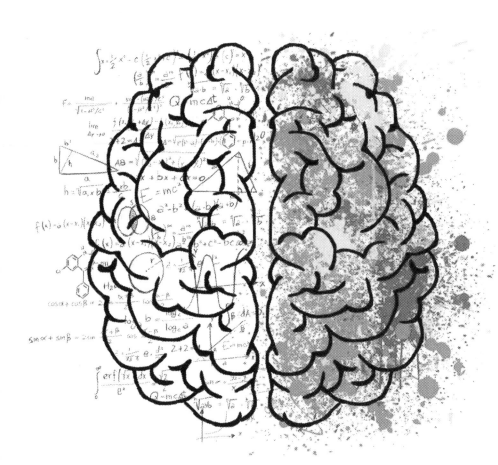

Live

Proprietary designs bring together hope,
peace and prosperity to the dime,

With each thought connecting and sharing perplexing
visions, with experiences and ideas intersecting.

These aspects will show how far one may grow,
allowing kings to flourish, paupers to nourish,
children o garnish and the forgotten reflourish.

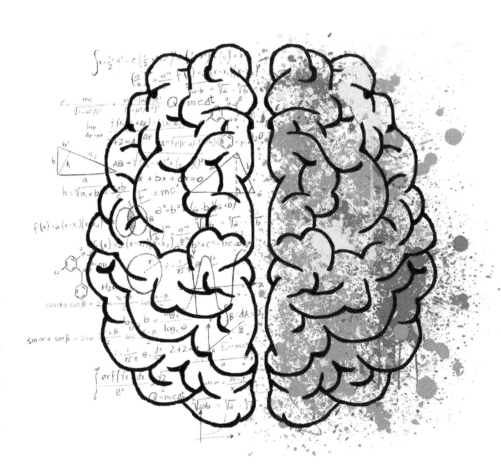

NECESSITIES

My chest feels tight and my mind feels numb,

Make it rhyme. Does it have to?

Dumb.

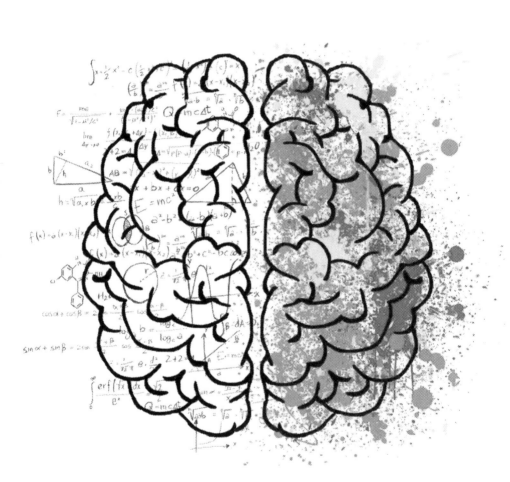

COERCION

In the deepest fathoms and the hard come-by truths,

There is desire and its counterpart,

Allowing for one to contemplate and graft their art.

The end of the beginning and the start of
the finished leaves ones worries to...

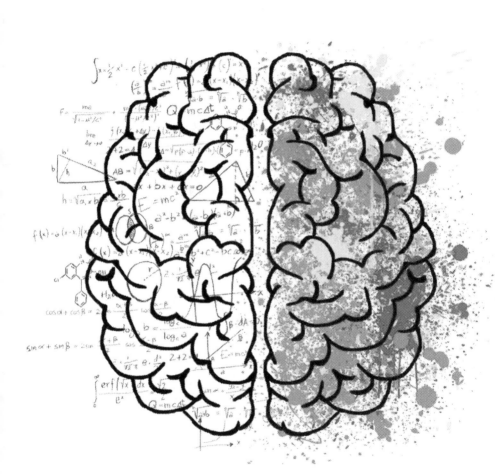

HAPPY

Fear and subterfuge may divert devotion

From this certain emotion,

Allow for room to partake,

With placement to return and mentalities to be protected.

Safeguard that which is wholesome.

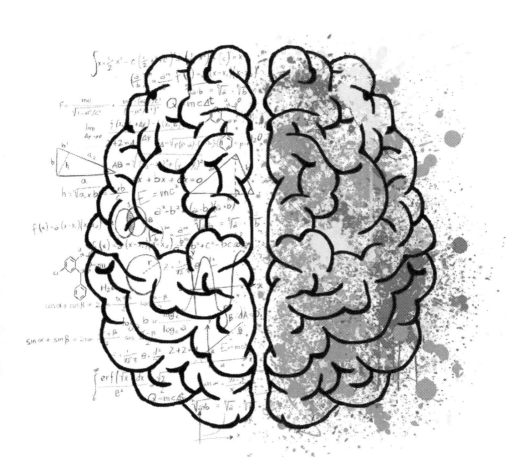

DEBUNKED

Nature and its intricate rhythming,

Defies our placement in existential swimming.

'In the beginning' they will say,

As this will contain our emotive brimming.

Fibonacci spirals and geometry,

Our beauty defined,

Bringing forth incredulous doubts
of the ascertained benign.

Accept and confer,

that which you can easily recognise from the

brilliant progenitor.

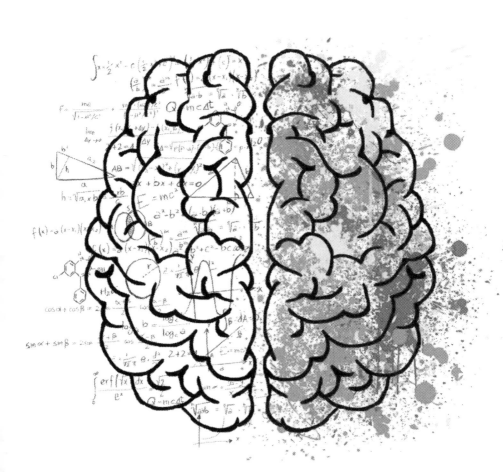

INTERLOPING

Crave for touch,

Entropy of the challenge,

Depiction of the trend,

coalition of the critical,

individuality of the paired.

Leaves loneliness in the throes of the romantical.

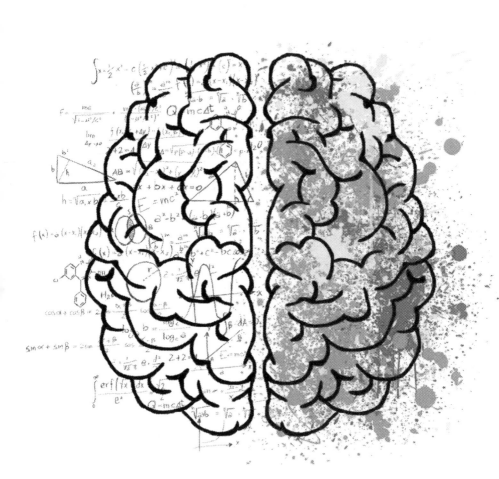

SHIVERS

One step,

Two step,

Quite the shock,

Three step,

Four step,

You hear a knock,

Five step,

Tick tock,

What is a sixth step?

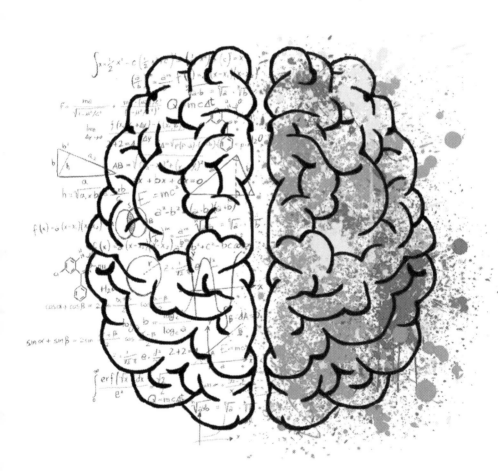

W5

Who, they asked.

What, they wondered.

Where, I answered.

When, was proclaimed.

Why, had pondered.

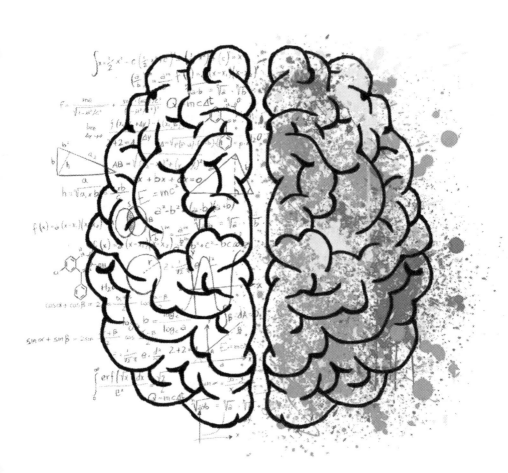

LIBERATION

One for the many,

One for the old,

One for the questioning,

One for the told,

One for the reverend,

One for the cold,

Many for the clever,

And some for the bold.

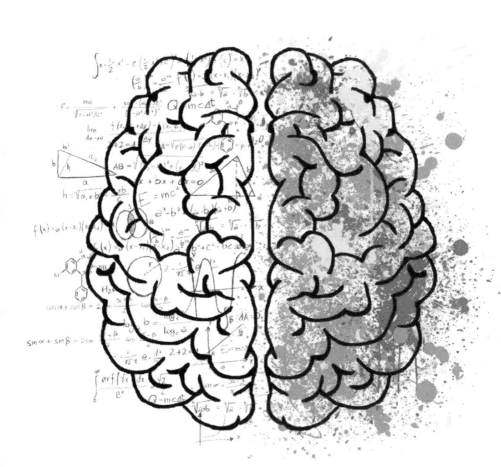

POP QUIZ

The first question,

Leaves room for the rudimentary…

Concluded by the elementary,

It continues,

Will it end.

Will it evolve.

Will it change.

Will it.

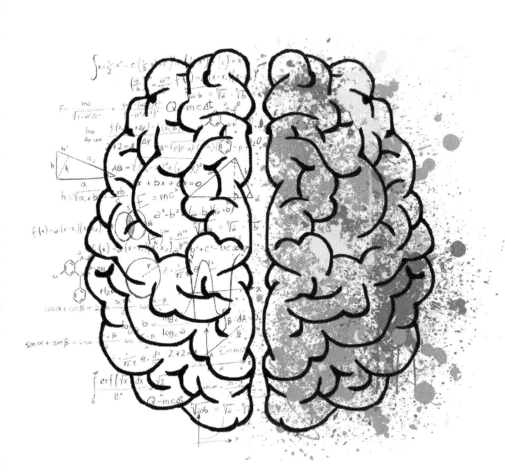

THE PENUMBRA

Shadows convey,

that which light relays,

the difference between nothing,

and the deliberation of something.

As perceivable as a crystal ball,

The mould of a mold,

Begs to differ.

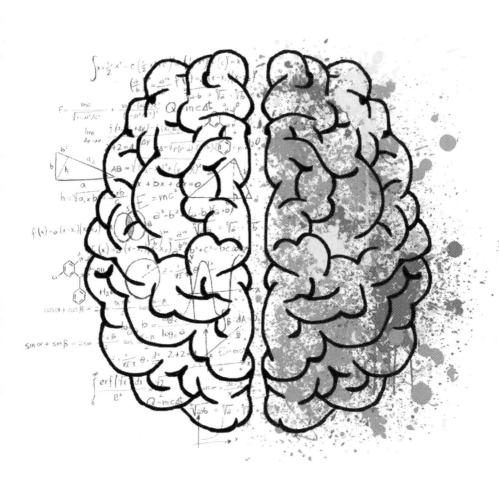

REFLECTION

Seil fi ereht, yaw a lliw ot tghuoseb eht tghuos,

?Dluow uoy

(If one could would they)

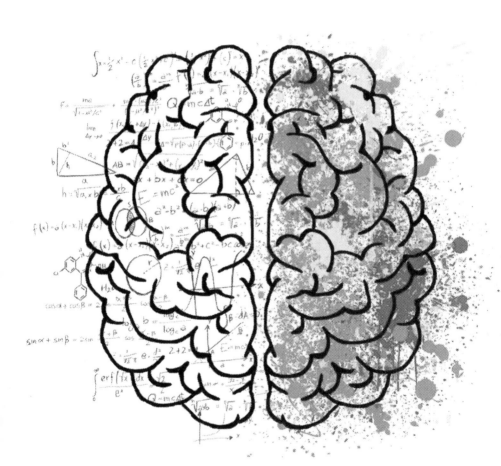

DEFLECTION

If, the instigator,

The difference between more & less,

And & or,

Maybe & therefore. (,)

Question its pretense.

(Questioned its pretense.)

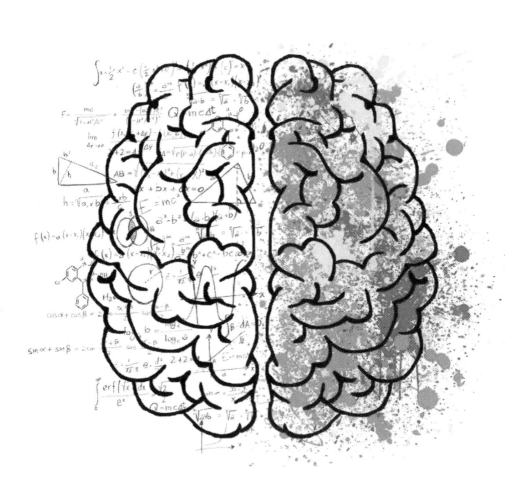

DISCOMBOBULATED

If then began with was,

There would be how,

ending with so,

The in between be built by some,

And layered with a drum,

Banging but, but, but.

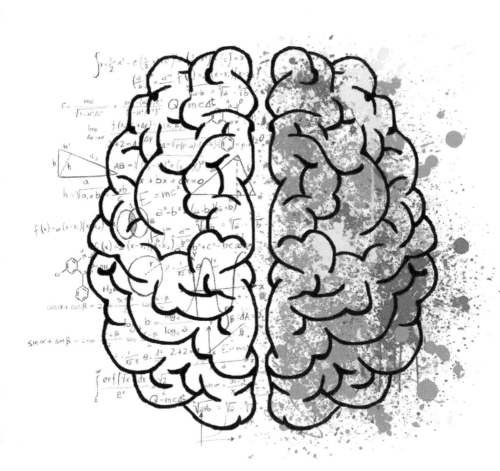

HISTORY

Is history written by the victors?

Children off to die,

Led by those nearest to it,

Distance be nothing but an apparition of spirit.

Qualms arisen to dictate the conflict,

Led to proportions of deficit.

Is history written by the victors?

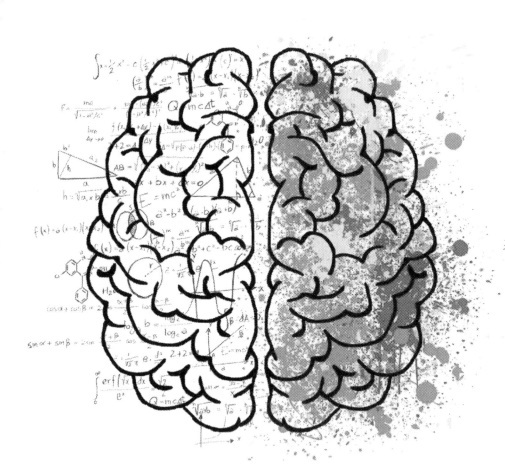

LAMENTATIONS

We cry,

Yet we seek,

We fall,

Yet we crawl,

We challenge,

Yet there's rebuttal.

Happy?

Deferred to Pandora,

Did curiosity kill the cat?

Or was Schrödinger the purveyor of its madness?

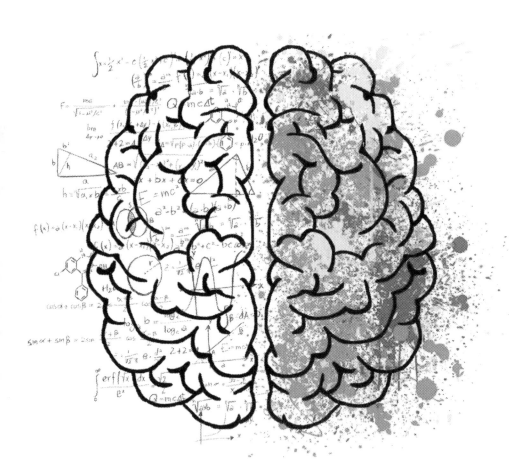

CONTENT

Content with content,

placidity,

happiness, the crux of enjoyment,

left to weather it delegates,

serotonin relinquished,

besieged on debates.

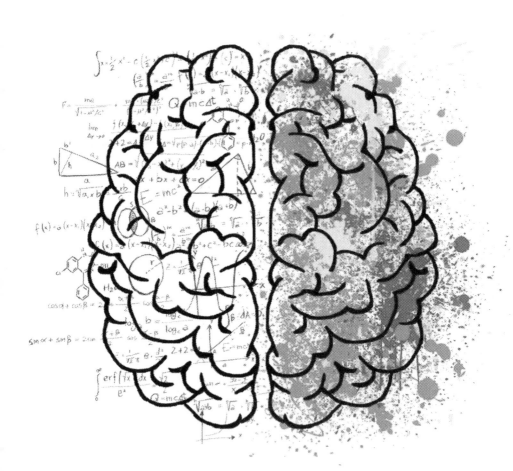

THROUGH FIRE & FLAMES

Strive,

Strive,

And further yet strive,

Complete your patrol through that which will incite a toll,

Continue your reparations,

Experience your contradictions,

Live out your propagations.

With honour one must partake,

and solidarity one may confide.

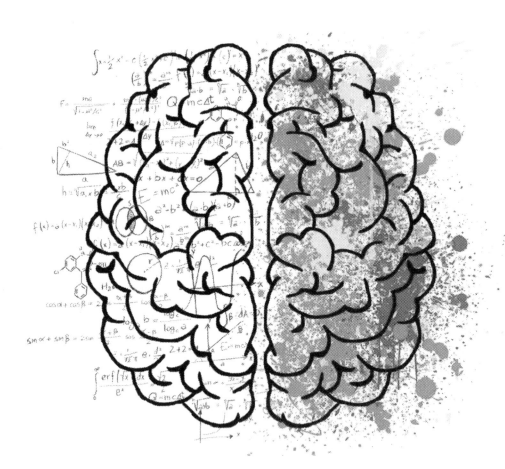

Constitution

Change,

let it be your motion,

Stasis,

Let it be your guide,

Confliction,

Let it be your growth,

Depravity,

Designate it your fears,

Honesty,

Complete your part.

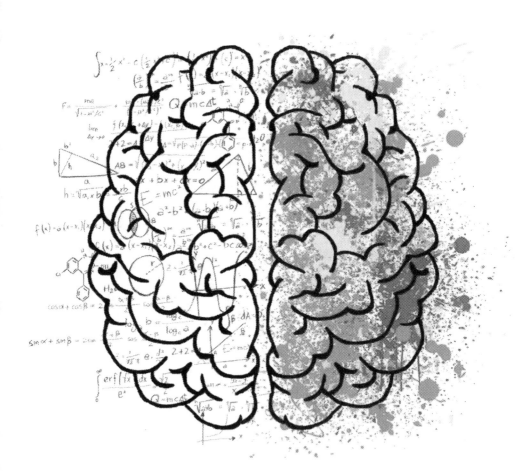

THE FATHOMS

Space and time,

Leagues in between,

Entire forces compete for relevance,

Their distances relegated in fathoms.

The fathoms of space incite large
distance and converge with time,

Allowing time it's spatial dictation arises
the quizzical philosophies of time.

We are of disparation as much as disparation is we.

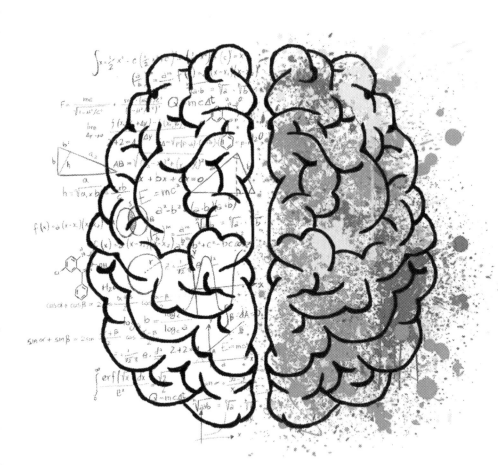

A Letter to You

You are the culmination of time,

Its faith in space,

Its belief in bewonderment,

Its total refinement of perfect.

Stay vigilant,

Remain unkempt,

Continue your constitution.

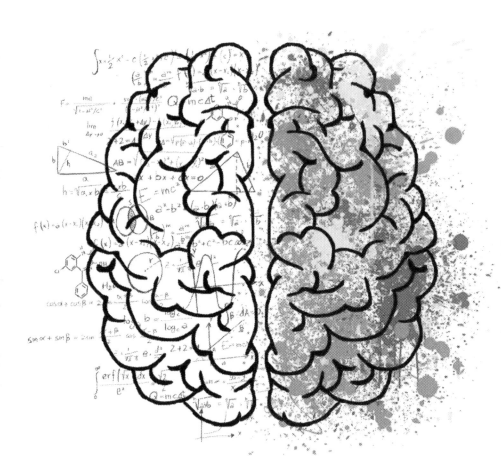

The End.

Do not fear,

Revere,

With contemplation,

Trust,

With fear,

Lust,

With confidence,

Embrace,

With expressionless diction,

Exclaim.

Printed in the United States
by Baker & Taylor Publisher Services